In Spite
of
Ourselves

Leah Papke

MILTON & HUGO L.L.C.
4407 Park Ave., Suite 5
Union City, NJ 07087, USA

Website: *www. miltonandhugo.com*
Hotline: *1- 888-778-0033*
Email: *info@miltonandhugo.com*

Ordering Information:
Quantity sales. Special discounts are granted to corporations, associations, and other organizations. For more information on these discounts, please reach out to the publisher using the contact information provided above.

Library of Congress Control Number: 2024914617
ISBN-13: 979-8-89285-224-1 [Paperback Edition]
979-8-89285-225-8 [Digital Edition]

Rev. date: 07/17/2024

Dedicated to you. I hope you find what you need here.

To know even one life has breathed
easier because you have lived;
This is to have succeeded.

—Ralph Waldo Emerson, "Success"

CONTENTS

Introduction

This poetry collection follows the chronology of a storyline, following the protagonist through the stages of life, represented as the plot. Each chapter explores the themes of self-identity, love, and loss which mature as the plot continues. "Anticipation," or the exposition, sets the plot by exploring the feelings of loss or lovelessness. Next, within the rising action, "Dream" fantasizes about a life with love. For the climax, "Frustration" capitalizes on the attempts at love and understanding and the devastations that follow. In the falling action, "Waking Up" identifies a new perspective on self-love. Lastly, "Redemption," or the resolution, brings everything together with a gratitude for it all. Ultimately, this is a story of how every protagonist can learn to thrive in spite of any disadvantages they may feel they have.

CHAPTER ONE

Anticipation

Inanimate World

Blurred vision
Fixated loosely
On an inanimate world.

Not wanting to adjust,
The haze is soft.

Sharpening the image
Doesn't add dimension
But still, we adjust.

Dilated eyes constricting
From an open mind
To reality.

What sharp objects.

Never more real
Or underwhelming.

Silence

Quiet now, dawn comes;
Though gloomy, another rises
Undivided
Another blink of the eye,
Ungiving rest.

How deep you must go
To know
The unloveable kind you are.
Push away,
It's all you know
The quiet

Quiet

The silence
Of a settled heart.
No longer tied
To fleeting love.

Silence
After a storm;

Blankets
After the cold;

Alone
In a big, empty home;

All you know
Is silence.

Nothing

My thoughts blur.
                    There is seldom a line of speech.
      All opinion transcends into a fuzzy silence.
                                 It's as black as a fading ripple:
                    Slow to none.
      Blockades, dams, walls, or what have you
                            Skyrocket the perimeter of thought
At any given chance.
      I can't think.
                         How treacherous my defenses have become.
No sense of my own,
                    Only configurations of what to be.

My mind hums the melody that the orchestra of mouths plays.

                    There is no more than noise with no end.

Nighttime

Since when did the sky turn black?

The switch was flipped and the stillness of the night has soaked up
the energy of the day.
The only movement comes from the trees slightly bouncing to the
falling rain.

Porch lights creep in the window casting shadows on the far wall.
Raindrops tap lightly on the door.

One car rattles by.
Headlights make the shadows run.

I want to run, too.

Gravity

Gravity is much lighter
When I'm not surrounded by it.

When I run and jump and fly
You could be fooled to think it was never there.

Until the moment I stop
I sit surrounded
And gravity puts his heavy hands upon me.

I look down at the world that I can never fly up from
Only ever getting feet higher.

The worst part is
Gravity never pushes me.
He just lets me know he'll hold me if I fall.

So sitting there, dangling my feet above the flood,
It comes down to my decision if I want to let go.

Environment

To endure the reality less preferred;
Awaking to the light of imperfection,
Walking the creaking house of disappointment,
Sleeping in the bed of defeat.
Another reality manifests itself in dreams.
Glimpses of hope hug reality;
A reminder of feeling more.

Lost

Without a home, you feel lost.

And lost isn't always a matter of not knowing which direction to go,
It's one of feeling like there's no right route,
That every way you take doesn't matter.

There's nowhere you need to be.
You don't need to be who you used to be or head where you were
heading.
There's anarchy around every corner you thoughtlessly explore.

With no direction, you're lost
Even when you know where you should be.

Lost in Your Freedom

A priceless pleasure
It is to feel free.
Take a left turn
Instead of right
Just to see.

But the thrill fades quickly
As the road goes on
When it's no longer dawn
But the dead of night.

Now this unfamiliar road
Loses its appeal.
The darkness makes you wonder:
Were you more in love with the ideal?

You have no one,
Not even yourself,
To hold you back.

Every inch is a mile,
The farther you go
The further gone you feel.

Where are you now?

Rain Boots

To dip your toe in the water is frightening,
It's not inviting.
Standing on the edge of solid ground
With one foot brave enough to feel the blue,
The shock shivers your nerves.

You used to love to swim.
Never have you been afraid of the rain.
It's courageous to dive in.
You'd hold your breath for so long underwater.
Thunderstorms only called for dancing outdoors.

The beads bounce off your coat and polish your skin.
It's only so long before your socks are soaked and each step is a
squish.

Go dry off.
Your skin is damp and frozen.
The chills run bone-deep.
There's water in your lungs.
The towel's already wet.
The logs have been out, you can't make a fire.
Your skin is no shield from the wind.

Now the waters seem comfortable.
A blanket to slip into.
You don't need to feel with your toe to know how safe it'd feel to sink
into your rain boots.

What Makes an Angel

Daylight flickers
Shadows run
Eyelashes deem a fuzzy filter

Rainbows turn from light
Sunshine on skin
Expose what's within

Shiny white lines
Escaping the complexion
The direction
Of the angel she is

Decorated purity
She's beauty's chaos
Agony surfaced
All from within

Summers spent hiding
Days spent dying
Cut wings cut skin

ASD

Leave everything you know at the door.
Step inside another world
Where the light fixtures glow a little brighter
And scratchy sweaters really itch.

Your voice is a boom box
And regular leather feels like screams to your fingertips.

Forget your language; your trains of thought.
Forget your schedule and all that you want.
Today, we're walking in another world; a different reality
Where all the little things
Were never as they seemed.

Blue Eyes

Blue eyes,
The ocean swells up in your eyes.
The rocky waves mock your calm surface;
They spit in your face.
You gulp.
Keep the murky waters suppressed.

Head and heart meet on the horizon line.
World upside down with your heart of clear skies.
Your head surges waves, chills daring toes.
You're the eye of your own storm.
Tell me why you're so cold.

Heart poured into the sea, adding chaos to it all.
It's a mess above and below.

We can't see the depth of your blue eyes.
Hurricane pupils.
Blackhole brain.

Blame the Stars

You're as far away as the moon.
You've disappeared so far into the realm of emotion
You forget that reality is an option.
It would be too easy.

When the moon waxes you swear you've got a grip.
It fills and for one whole night, you might not feel so empty.
So you enjoy it while it lasts.

You live to love and give,
But you give more than you have
And you love all the wrong things.

All you want is a home.
They'll take you anywhere with all you have to give,
But can you ever feel like you belong in a realm outside of your own?

Empathy

Living a thousand lives
Through the people I've loved
Met on the streets
Passed by in rushing cars
Glimpses through windshields
Rear views
Television shows.

I've enabled heartbreak –
Broke my other halves
Breaking myself the same
Both extremes felt deeply
In my heart which landscapes the breathing world.

A Day

Tired
Irritated
Barely awake.

Pain
Nausea
My body hurts.

Upset
Sad
Exhausted
Mad.
Annoyed
Relaxed
Focused
Stressed.
Accomplished
Mess
Rushing
Out the door.

Anxious
Control
Nervous
At peace
Scared
Safe
I made it to work.

Awkward
Aware
Now get to work.

Affable
Smiley
They lighten my day.

Tuned-in
Alert
Excelling
Alright.
Hunger
Fatigue
Dread
Discouraged.
Reminded
Resilient
Rewired
Returning.

On break
Searching
Driving
Learning.

Alone
Independent
Serene
Fulfilling.
Rushing
Through traffic
Back in
Abruptly.

Dragging
Slowly
Progressing
Through papers.

Smiling
Laughing
Wits and humor.

Happy
Bonding
Open
Accepting.

Loving
Belonging
Lingering
Sorrow.
I'll see you tomorrow.

I Thought I Was Dreaming

No one's really with me, they're just there.

I walk away from the world I stand aloof to,
From the people I know better
Than they will ever know themselves.
I tuck myself in and tell myself goodnight.

I go off to a loosely put-together reality
Where I watch every purposeful person
Walk the streets and love their home.

I stand and stare at the scene
Feeling like the audience intruding.
Out of place but never in the way,
Notably wrong if noted at all.

I wake up from the illusion,
Bedsheets hugging my back
And the awareness of myself
Spreading from my core.

I wake up but I feel the same.
No one's really with me, they're just there.

Lighthouse

Peering over the dark sea, it's always scared me
And it feels like everyone wants to intrude to shore.

Building walls but searching for something to let in.
I build higher and higher to get a better look,
To see if I can ever find something worth getting to me.

Patrolling every voyager wandering near,
The people lose their dimension with these heights.
They'll never reach me up here
Not from what I can see.

CHAPTER TWO

Dream

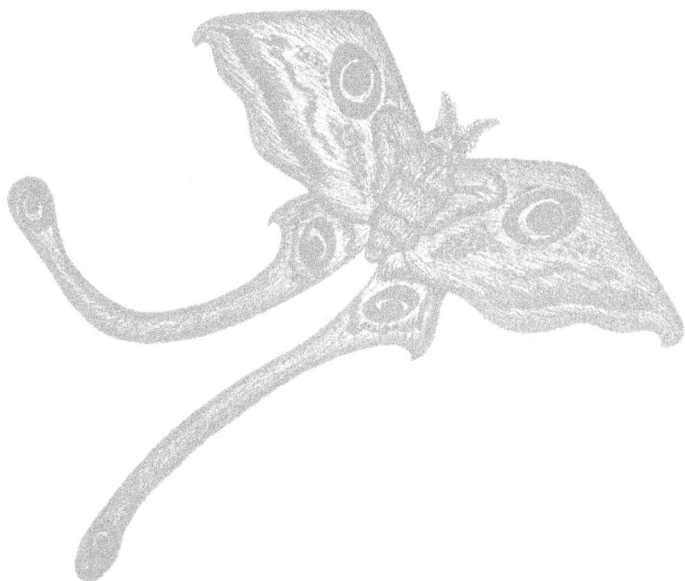

Expression

If I could paint
The act of Adam
Being ridden of his rib
And a single angel
Wallowing around
Looking for her founder,
I would.

If I could demonstrate
On a canvas
The desire
To come home to you,
My studio would be full
Of epic scenes,
Portraits hung up
Leaning against every wall
I remain closed into.

If I could just
Express
How it feels
To be in longing,
I would do anything.

I'd go as far
As to write a book about you,
Alluding each line of poetry
To every way you make me feel.

The Point of No Return

We collided
On a late-night
In a crowd of strangers I vaguely know.

It was your eyes
That scared me most.
I was shy for them
To see me.

The idea of you
Chased away
By your overwhelming
Humanness
And complications.
Suddenly more real
Than ever before.
Three dimensional
And complex
Opinionated
And motivated
Carrying secrets
Of your own.

Would this be it?
The breaking of the ice.
The point of no return:
Your eyes meet mine.

But we never really met.

You were there
Just so far away
Because I ran
From what could be.

Lace of Love

I've felt love once before you
In the sweet pain that's laced with love
The forehead kiss that melts you
Makes you tighten your brows before you almost weep

Empty Lungs

I stopped breathing at the sight of you
And my heart fell right through my chest
Into empty lungs.

Breathless, thudding heart, surrendered to you.
My breath you'd breathe, sedating a smile, exulting coughs of
laughter.
I'd rip out more of myself to give you my all.

Your delicate face shines; illuminating the light within your precious
soul.
In your presence, the world stops spinning,
For a moment we were infinite.

You ceased the breath from out my lungs
And crafted the bleeding air into a beautiful array.

Pray You Here

On the days that are long
And in the exaggerated hours
Before sleep,
I pray you here
To lay with me.

The last I saw your face
Was weeks ago
Here in the same place.
I pray you stay on my mind tonight.

Too bitter of the sweet
To have you only
In my dreams.
Some sweet relief from longing
Blurred out by my sleepy brain.

When I wake I know you came,
That we spent some time together,
And I'll carry that
Into the next day
Hoping to dream the same.

Every Day This Year

Each time I wake,
My mind turns on
And turns to you.

Like sunshine on skin
My open windows bring in
Inescapable thoughts of you.

Now sometimes
You never leave;
I relive desire in my dreams.

When I wake,
If you give it time,
You've become the first thing on my mind
Each and every day this year.

We're Better in My Dreams

I find you there
Innocent and forgiving,
Perfect and flawless,
So you stay with me at night
Sleeping with me still
But you won't remember my dreams.

I'm happy when I sleep
And see you're there.
We're better than happy to not,
In love to not.
We embrace it with no fear,
But my dreams are only my feelings.

Your dreams are different.
We're different people –
We've talked about this already.
The reunion kisses
And subconscious apologies
Fade in the morning with you.

Rather Dream

My dreams of you are so pleasant –
Memories of a life unlived.
Frozen time, intimate eyes, all I see is you and I.
Alone together, a world created.

We are so close, so understood.
Our tongues meet like the grounding of a plane to track
And I know
If our heads were ever too far off, we've come right back.

A life full of visions
Brought together in this collision
To know the differences between us is infinite
Yet thin.

Engulfed in each other –
I only know love from my dreams.
The man you are won't know
Half of me when we wake,
But the memory of what never happens
Hides low in my mind
Waiting for the time
Love can transpire
In real life.

Withholding passion from reality –
Wanting more than you give me –
I rather dream.

Come Back

You're on the list of people
I'm hoping will one day come back;
The few who resurface and recycle
Into my thoughts and scattered consciousness.

I think of the times I've missed you,
And I begin to count the times of longing
As moments with you.
You've never left my heart.

In my head I relive
The best days of my life
Where you're with me each time.

I think about those stupid moments
Where I didn't know how much you meant to me
And I think about maybe telling you this time
If there ever comes one,
If I can truly express how I feel.

I've played it out a million times
Different scenes and settings
Taking on days and nights:

First, we talk about how
We never wanted to lose touch at all.
We tell each other that
We've been wishing the best for one another
And we're happy the other has found
Their way back into our lives.

We've created a really sturdy foundation,
Now that we've gone with and without.
Now that we know better than to leave,
It's no longer an option.

We're good together.
I don't want to be without.

I'm hoping one day you'll come back.

Opportunity

Finally, I saw you.

It went too quickly for all that I've been holding on to.
All that I've been hoping for.

Some part of me wanted so badly for these circumstances to occur.
Another thought it was best left as is.

But then your face glew subtly in the crowd of strangers.
You fit right in with the busy people I'll never be.
I'd imagine it almost looked like a normal encounter.
A friend to a friend.

How long were you looking before you spoke up?
I wonder what those strangers thought of us.
I wonder if anyone even noticed.

Each thought of mine unleashed as the door closed.
I couldn't think for the next hour besides what I should have said.
Yet you left.
And I left you with no answers.
I gave you a blank face with wide eyes.
I left you with nothing when I had so much to give.

I watched you leave once again.

Man

God created man:
He made you
Ever so lovely
And strange
And lonesome.

He made you,
This universe,
Infinite paths,
Yet we met.

Walking adjacent
I watch you live
I want to watch you breathe
But you'll never get that close to me.

The narrow path grows
Rocks and dust and bugs
I see us running this road together
But you're miles ahead.

Empty Chair

Once I knew you could be
The one to take care of me
I arranged room to keep you,
Setting up a place to stay in my brain.

A dinner table
A loveseat
A queen-size bed.

I made up this home to hold you,
I made it look its best.

Each day I'd wake with the anticipation
Shortly followed by frustration
That I still sit alone.

The bed is too big to hold my half a heart,
The extra chair serves no purpose,
And the table is set for someone who will never come home.

Mirror

You left a mirror
On the left side of my bed
Where your warm skin sent heat
Through the sheets

Now it's cold.

A creepy, haunting cold
Coming from the mirror.

Just me
Just me
Here alone.

It's so cold in this room.

Everything is bigger
I feel smaller.

I hate what you left me.

Vulnerability

Showing my weaknesses
Used to show me our strength;
The trust in you
To never want to harm.

Bonding over the fragility
Of our delicate nature,
You held me safely
Away from myself.

Now every innocent confession
Comes back to bite.
You use your words as a weapon
And Lord knows I don't want to fight.

So go ahead and shoot
Right where you know you should.
And I'll have nothing left to say
Because you already know
How much it hurts.

The Puppeteer

In your thought
I am flooded.
Drenched by the feelings
You unconsciously give.

You've met me
Deep in my psyche
Where no one before
Has traveled so far.

In the core of me
My idea of you lies;
Dwelling in the heart
Of my guarded mind.

The wind blows
And a gust of you arises
Engulfing me
Further into you.

One cannot deny
The strategy
Of getting overthrown.

By the give in my heart
You came in sweetly
And stuck your ground.

Now your presence roams
Fulfilling and straining
The crack in my heart
You came in by.

And I'll call you the puppeteer
For the way you pull
At the strings of my heart.
Never will you know
What you evoke.

Maybe One Day

I want to see how the setting sun
Shines its soft orange
Onto the rosy complexion of your face.
Your golden skin tone
Would warm the atmosphere;
The prettiest color there may ever be.

What contentedness I'd feel
Sitting passenger in your car
Hearing your music play,
Hearing who you are.

The windows are down
And so is your guard
And for a moment I think:
This is who we're meant to be.

And when we get back to your place
You'd hold me, and I'd feel at home:
To be there with you
To look around your room
Seeing all the things that make you.

And like a puzzle, I'd keep busy
Putting together those pieces
While your voice sings to me
In elevation of excitement
As you begin to ramble about your passions.
Your words fill my heart beyond what I ever knew.

All I want is to stand beside you
And tilt my head upward to meet your eyes.
Because we're two lone souls
But there's so much of us in each other.

So maybe one day
Your hand could be with mine
And I'd know instead of wonder
What it's like to be with you.

Never Could Have

You dangled the world right in front of me.
On a string, you held everything I've never had.
You reached out your hand and offered my dreams.
Like the Creation of Adam, our fingertips never touched.
Somewhere in it all, you got lost in my dreams.
You became both what I had and what I never could.

Ghosts

They say ghosts will come back
To haunt or wallow,
Hovering over unfinished business
Or those whom they hold a grudge.

Though I've never understood
The dead's need to linger,
I sit tonight in the evening moonlight
Across my high school football stadium.

How many years has it been now
I wonder as it strikes me:
My time is dead here
As am I to it

Yet I wallow in what could have been
If only I had been more.

Why Dream

Why do these dreams taunt me the same?
Ones of apologies and love that no longer remains
A glimpse of reality's hope
Festers in my forebrain
Swallowed by conscious thought
Never rational enough
Until I sleep and it releases
The hope seeps and squeezes
Through areas of memories
And emotions while my sleepy brain
Stands vulnerable to Hope's intrusion
Now I think I really feel
That you came back
We had that conversation
Just like I hoped
It went how I suppose I always thought it would
And I wake
Goddamnit I wake
To nothing but the same
Taunted change
Hopeless reality
You and I are still the same.

Paint with Words

If one can paint with words
And the alphabet lies swirled in a canister with a brush,
The color blue would smear a long line
Along the atmosphere of us.

CHAPTER THREE

Frustration

Rain

I fell in love with Rain.
Once the clouds claimed my Earth,
I knew I was in for some change.

Rain was different for me,
The darker clouds rendered more concrete.
There was something about what deepness
That lay amidst the wandering conqueror.
Dark, rich, deep.

He met me there:
Where the summoned winds pushed me to.
Alone on the canvas of Earth,
Rain opened up to me.
He held my hand,
Kissed my cheek,
And wrapped me in unfamiliar matter.

The sun stood back and watched him fall for me,
And I fell back.

It wasn't until I laid in the mud
Did he leave with a promise to be back.
So, I watched myself dry
As the sun took me in.
What beautiful timing for my love to return,
Bearing showers of love
And thunderous applause.

To the chaotic love, I danced until I swam
Until I choked.
My love could not hear me under his wrath.
I became it.

The wind came back to guide me,
But pushed me further into a drown.

My love did not know my cries are not his language –
That water down the throat and out of the eyes means "help."

My love lost me in a storm of good intentions.

Misunderstood

I want you to see me,
So I show you my all;
The parts of myself I can't quite name,
Yet you do.

You tell me it's nothing,
Or that I'm okay,
But I'm not.
And you don't see that.
You don't see me at all.

This darkness is eating me alive,
But you call it fine
Because you don't *understand.*

You never will.

Wreckage

Our time was handcrafted
By history and each other force
That fell into place by fault.

The gravity of circumstances
Aligned wreckage to live for.
Every mistake built a bandaged stairway
To which I stumbled over countless times.

Pulling myself over the ambiguity
Grappling onto the uncertainty
Clawing into the crumbling rise of action,
I found you only feet up.

Finding thrill in the sidetracked climb
I swept away the wreckage to make shelter.
The dust covered over, and direction was no matter.
Digging in the dirt we shared time together,
Aiding one another in the dark.

Breakthroughs of sunbeams and life beneath the surface shouted
victories.
There was strength passed onto each other to carry on,
There was fighting when we needed it back,
There was never light at the end of the dreams we burrowed.

We wrestled in the cave we made,
Battle cries cracked the safe haven
Walls made from ash collapsed
Disillusionment was mistaken for hope.

With lungs full of smoke, I trudged onwards.
The escape was only back into the fogged ground.
Atop piles of wreckage, I heaved onto what seemed next
But every inch proved twice as hard
The farther I moved from you.

There was never a compass,
Charcoal and fool's gold were hidden treasures in the disarray.
Belly down on grey matter.
Body mixed with dust.

The Devil Came Home

After a brief getaway
Setting up captives
In his hellish graves,
He came home to me,
Pushed past me on his way in,
Kicked off his shoes,
And let his reign begin.

He knocked over tables,
Shattered all the glass,
Broke everything I put my heart into,
And rubbed it in.

He told me that my soul was his vessel,
That God wished for a way in,
But he bargained for it,
Saying he'd spare others just to have me.

Sunflower

Follow me beside the field
Mind the thick stocks and heavy flowers.
Sunflowers climb just overhead.

They tower us.
Some look down and watch you leave.
Others pay no sight to the chaos to come.

The sun shines down
Casting shadows between the leaves.
The edge of the field bordered with beauty.

What lies behind lies behind.
The corner is turned to approach the end.
A flower mocks the sun's shape – a shadow of itself.

Here it is, where I stand, watching the silhouettes dance.
You never turn the corner to see it.
Time ticks by with each passing car and gust of wind.

Sun beats down, beating me alone.
I turn back, sure you were not there.
Not around this corner or the next or the next or the next.

Circles around the square field again and again.
You were there.
You were there.

1,000,000 to 1, the stocks stand tall as I fall.
You emerged from the field with tears in your eyes.
There was nothing in there but your own mind.

Anticipating

I remember watching you
From outside the bedroom window.
The car pulled into the driveway
When you jumped out and laughed.

Your friends played their music
And life filled the air.
I peered over the snowy scenery
To watch you walk inside.

For a moment I wait
Anticipating your call
But I never heard my name.

I watched you walk back out
Only moments gone by
To hop back into your car
And busy life.

Incompletion

What are we doing
Stuck in silence
Screaming for one another
Lightyears away

We're running
Faster than ever
In the only direction
That has ever mattered

Wanting change
Petrified to make it
Never colliding
Suffering incompletion

Yearning for one another
Needing comfort
From the stranger
We've been loving
From a distance

Each move I make
You change the game
Stuck in stalemate
Getting to know you
In retrograde

Overpowered

Overpowering night accepts defeat by the light behind your eyes.
Together, we are radiant dawn to dusk; on my own, I am lost.

Overpowering depression accepts defeat by the power of your wide
smile.
The thoughts of death dissolve when I am yours.

Overpowering loss consumes me — it cannot be defeated: you're not
here to save me.
Gleaming lights descend to hell — they light up our future —
together or separate.

Overpowering guilt consumes me.
Overpowering darkness intrudes me.
Overpowering love corrupts my perception.

To Find Love

Is there more to life than love?

Do the flashy, gold-speckled daydreams of
Consoling
Completion
Paired solitude catering safety
Derive from ignorance
Innocence
Nativity
Even helplessness?

Do we need a love to save us?
Will there ever be such a thing?

The inevitability of heartbreak
Loss
Destruction
Delusion
Yet we still fight.
Why do we still fight?

Perhaps the genuine life of love
Is an outright lie
Taught to confide —
Like faith taught to children —
To give them hope of resurrection
To the grave we all dig,
But lovely more
With hope of salvation:

To find love
When there is no love to find.

Strangers, Again

From friend
To friend
To friend
I look across the hall and smile.

Recognition, and I smile.
Recognition, and I stop.

It's your face I see —
A friendly face
Feeling the same familiarity —
Before my memory recollects
And recalls the disappointment
Associated with those eyes.

I wonder if you could see my heart break
All over again
In that moment?
Hope to despair
Nested behind my eyes.

We look away
And walk by.

Lunch Box

The lunch box I used
When we lived together:
"Bentgo."

We got it at Costco.
"Bentgo,"
I say to myself at 7 am
Peering into my kitchen cabinet,
And your eyes
From the night before
Flash back into my head.

A dream with you
Holding me,
Just holding me,
And no more.

"Don't kiss me,"
I tell you,
"I've moved on from you."

Yet, in the dream,
You were holding me
Like I yearned the proximity
But not the intimacy.

We were close
But never close.
I will never trust you
With my heart.

The Guilt of Dissonance

Debating subjectivity
Turning away the validation of uncertainty.
Isn't that certain enough?

Love is bitter
Loss can be sweet.
Isn't that certain enough?

This purgatory state of indecision:
Wallowing in the paradox of hope –
Anticipating the fall off the edge
Eyes glued to the floor
One foot out the door.
Isn't that certain enough?

But the love that we share
The love, the love!
Isn't *that* certain enough?

Torturing the partner
Who chooses to stay.
Explaining feelings away.
Who's right, who's wrong,
Is anybody certain at all?

Company

Lifeless people
Occupy my mind
Known to brief degrees
Meaning the world to me
Keeping me company
In my lonely head

The more people I meet
The less each means to me

Incoherent faith
Fleeing love
All opportunity amounting
On what could be

I will make you
King of my mind
Ruler of my time
Dictate me lies
Until I realize
You don't deserve it

Stretching meaning
Factualising fallacies
I'll make the most
Out of you and me
Until I alone
Mean something to me.

Only a Mirror

You're talking to my facade.
You converse with my shiny shell.
You'll laugh with my comedic front.
You know no more than your mirror
And I can tell you everything you see in me
Has nothing to do with who I am.

Different Worlds

I live in different worlds
Different perspectives
With different people
Who think different things.

I am a wanderer
I am lost
I am pathetic
I am adventurous
When I walk the streets
Or a small path in the woods.

I am educated
I am naive
I am stuck-up
I am sweet
When I walk to my car
Eyes peering through their blinds.

I am alone
I must think I'm alone
I am safe
I am in danger
As I lay with eyes up towards the sky.
Eyes eyeing mine.

I am running
I am scared
I am stupid
I am getting nowhere
When I wrestle with myself
And struggle for the truth.

Theory of Mind

I have this hunch
This theory of mine
That won't let me sleep
Eat walk turn run look be
Without seeing myself
For what you might see.

It doesn't come as a reminder
Because it never leaves
This theory of mine.

How do you see me?

Perplexing reflections
Your eyes my eyes her eyes their eyes
Different different different different.

My eyes grow sleepy
With hysteria or delusion;
This theory of mind
Has set in long ago.

When, may I ask, does the dust settle?
When do I see myself
Correctly, properly, if ever?

To close the gap
Of dissonance
Confusion
Discrepancy,
I know I need to see myself
Through me.

When will I be?

Truly Sad

Am I not being true to myself
When I enjoy the breeze,
Run in the sand,
And laugh along with new old friends?

Am I deceitful
When I smile at the sunlight,
Get tickled by sweet reality?

I feel like a liar
A loser
When I am happy
Only to be reminded
That it is something that I am not.

I convince myself of a smile
Holding it tightly for hours
Before the hurt overbears
And I begin to cry
Confessing to myself
I am sad.

Cravings

Will the attraction to disparities —
The dark side of the moon
A lonesome howl
An aching heart
With my lover on the other side of the bed —
Will these tastes
Ever leave my tongue?

Will these cravings
Flee my mind?

Like bad habits
Gone
They knock
Just to remind.

Conscious choices
Daily decisions
The life I'm making
After you.

Making You

He redefined me in a single instant. He shouldn't have made me.

What's Inside

He could only get inside of me if he pulled me open and ripped me apart.
And so he did.

Selfish

I'm choking
Gagging
When I try to
Stomach you
And what you've done.

I lean over the sink
Thinking I'm sick
At the thought of you
The feelings of you.

Your actions linger
In my gut
And twist my insides
Sharply.

The betrayal of you
Clenches my heartstrings
And suffocates my heart
As it unwillingly beats on.

My lungs have been slit
Like tires
In a rage response

And I struggle to breathe
In a breath
Of this polluted world.

I feel like a ragdoll
Tossed around and beaten
By your selfish ways.

Ignorance

You don't see
Fresh wounds
Drying blood
Aching skin

Guilt
Shame
Hate

Time has past
I have grown
Sowing each stitch
Together on my own

Now I'm clean
Healed
Scarred

The shiny traces aren't quiet
They start beating
Breathing
With a hunger

A desire

To destroy myself
To break myself
To hate myself

Breathing slowly
Hibernating under my skin
Breathe in

Go away

One-Sided

I can love you when the lights go low,
When the feeble words on a serpent's tongue mean enough.

I can love you when it's easy, when all you want is touch.
I can provide all you need as long as you're here with me.

We can walk together on this road and ignore every backward step
we take.
Let's laugh together, masked in ignorance, like this'll be forever.

You'll hold me through the night, passed out drunk and fine,
But you should know that my heart has turned on you as my back
where we lay.

I'll hold it all against you, but never to you, for you just don't know.
It's much better to love what's easy, to love someone you'll never
know.

Familiarity

He felt like home.
Never mind the haunting loneliness,
The familiarity of suffering,
The quiet nights alone under a roof of people.

He felt like the warm bed
Which would hold me on the peaceful nights
And the uncomfort
Of tossing and turning
In a place I don't belong.

His cold shoulder held my head like slammed doors,
Denial like siblings screaming,
Misunderstandings like forced communication.

So, to me, he felt like home.

Beetle

I think irony is my favorite kind of humor;
As a matter of fact, I know.

Thoughtless acts like the call to save
A drowning beetle
Belly up
As I stroll through the clear-set water.

A fallen flower floats nearby:
An opportune lifesaver.

With the current from a human hand
The relentless beetle climbs aboard,
Tired, I'd imagine, from struggling
Upside down in an open stroke.

Climb on, rest, there you go.
Back to wherever you may go.
I smile, swim away.
It's better this way.

My mother, moments later, notices
Its new home rests on her raft.
She draws back, makes a face,
Then smash.
She scrapes off the bug onto the cement.

I don't stop her.
I can't.
It hurts, but I laugh.

Estranged

Does it scare you
To not know either child,
To house strangers —
Enemies —
Embodiments of yourself?

Does it terrify you
That you don't know where either daughter goes
To rest
To live on away from you?

Does it sadden you
To know they hadn't wanted to leave
But, rather, felt pushed away?
Or, do you think of it differently?
Knowing you did all you could.

Family

Building off the ruins can work.
We can use pieces of what's left behind.
Crumbled architecture and cracked foundations,
We could build a palace here.
The land is nice, it must have been perfect
In its prime.
I sit sometimes, in the center of it all,
Flat ground with hills and valleys,
And I think of the potential of this place.

Child-like imagination
I grew up in this castle.
The chandeliers painted rainbows within the doors.
Birds would sing to us through the walls.
Soft rain tapped on my ceiling
And I'd slowly fall asleep.
In my sleep is where I wake
To find puddles wanting to entrap me
Birds shouting at me to leave
And rainbows washing away with the rain.

We've ruined the supplies we never even used.
This place really could have been nice.
Pillars like virtues, all crumbled in their attempt.
To find where I went wrong
Seems all I can do,
Yet I can't make anything more
Out of these ruins.

You Were There/Director Eyes

You were there when it fell apart, when I did.
You were the bright eyes that followed the destruction from scene to
scene.
You watched the context piece together, stayed through the conflict,
were there at the climax.
Scenes fade black the nights you didn't stay.
Your director's eyes only took in what you believed, you never saw
behind the scenes.
When you play it back, if you ever press rewind, I want to know what
you find.
Can you trace back the meaning of all these scenes?
Do the characters that mean so much to me mean anything to you?
Did you want to be a character, too,
Anything more than just director's eyes?
When we fell apart, the action did too.
The closure came after you left.
So now that we've met our end I ask:
What does this story mean to you?

Over

And then it was all over, just like we had always seen coming.
You still live on your own.
I still live with my parents.
And I know both lonely places feel how they've always felt, before you and I, and now after.
We knew this was coming.
It was something to fear, but is this really that scary: normalcy?
We knew what we had was a privilege – one of those temporary vacations.
Every morning spent waking next to you was another tally on the wall to our unsuspecting release from one another.
How long until this dream falls apart, we wondered.
Will we finish the narrative before waking softly to the daylight, or would a loud crash startle us out of this deep daydream?
It seems the dream of you and I faded into reality before into nothing.
From a perfect love, to a real love, to skepticism, to the breakup.
A smooth transition.
I wasn't afraid.
But the final decision to let go was prolonged.
I wanted to wait, to stay in the purgatory of lost hope before it was concrete, to live in the maybe.

I know this tortured you, along with every other back-and-forth leap
I'd make regarding our love.
I had a teetering faith in us.
To lift you up and then down, give you hope to preface fear, and leave
you paralyzed by uncertainty.
Your safe haven in me became a bunker to dwell on fight or flight.
I'm sorry.
After it all, though, I must admit this is what I always saw.
There is no bias in the hindsight of our love never sitting right.
The begging for a change was no mishap.
I couldn't keep going.
I couldn't love you like you deserved.
You couldn't do the same for me.
We were at a stalemate.

Sharp Knife

Without you now
A breath
Fresh air
Humanness
Individuality.

Without you now
An ache
In my back
Where you stabbed.
Unwillingness to trust
To forget.
Anger
With you.

Without you now
A knife
In my heart.
Loneliness
Isolation
Wanting.

I simply ache
On all sides
With or without.

You are not the knife
Just who I've assigned the weapon to.

Yinyang

I've felt before like a bad man,
That there's evil lurking deep in the parts of me
That no one can quite see.

I've felt surges of rage and anger
That I can't quite dismiss as okay.
I've done things that I cannot condone.

Moments I've endured that make my frail stomach wheeze, disgusted
in myself.
And they playback when I wish to be good,
Almost as a reminder that I might never change.

I've done wrong, I can admit.
I've been wrong, I am too often.
I've said and done things I wish I hadn't.
I've sinned and sinned again.

But if I'm so evil, so bad because of these
How come I wish to be more?

As I Was

Does the 'me' you know
Still dance around —
Gitty at life
Flying birds
The rising sun —
Alive, still, in your mind?

Does she arise and snap
Irritated at your misunderstanding
Angry with her mistrust in you,
Or has she calmed
Has she grown,
Has she become the 'me'
You'll never know?

Remember

I cannot remember you.
Your eyes like a long-ago-seen photo
Lips just a shape
A mystery of touch.

I cannot remember your hands
Which we held
Hours accumulated
With you in me.

I cannot imagine a conversation
With you then
With what we know now.

Not until I hear the music—
Bringing back
Feelings at the time—
Is when you come back to my mind
For the first time in 6 months.

I welcome your memory
And I question it.

Cruel

The world doesn't have a cradle
For my soft heart
Or a silver spoon
To feed me love.

It doesn't rotate toward the sun
For my chilling skin.
It doesn't hold its rain
From my soaking face.

The world cannot bear
A life so fragile.

The evolution brought upon
Thick skin
Cold, quiet lips,
And eyes to trap the soul behind.

I hang heavy and low
Living slow
Loving hard and excruciatingly long.

My body shames me
For carrying around such a weight –
A useless weight –
Behind my chest;
Such a burden
Behind my eyes.

The world was not meant for me.

Samaritan Eyes

How did you end up here?
The empty lot of land
Where one freeway meets another.

Drivers slow at the light
From 70 miles per hour
Back to the pace of man
For one red light
Before they're gone.

You can't leave
It seems
You've come by foot
From afar
Probably not sure where to go from here.

You stand at the street corner
"Testing human kindness"
Like you're only made to be that.

You are so much more
But the hands of grief
Weigh you down
As you search desperately
For a Samaritan's eyes.

I swear I could see the blue
Of yours
From down the line
Of cars waiting to pass you.

We stared at one another
And I think you knew
I would be one of the only
To want to help you.

I didn't have to say anything
Because the eyes always say it all
So you came to me genuinely
And said, "Thank you so much, sweetie."

I looked into your Samaritan eyes
Wondering how it is you've gotten here
And I hope you heard everything else
I meant to tell you
Before I told you, "Please, take care."

Deeds

I remember visiting Detroit as a kid.
From dinner, my family and I
Walked the night's streets.
I turned the city corner to find
A dollar running with the wind.
It's a crazy thrill when you're young,
Both luck and fortune.

I held it for some time before walking by
A woman pressed against a brick wall.
Covered in blankets on the street,
It was cold and windy and no place to be.

I turned towards my mom to ask
If I could give her my dollar that I had found.
She surprised me when she said I could.

I approached the dark face, apart of the shadows.
Her eyes glowed a strong white.
Large and tired and aware.
Blankets hid her body.
I looked down at her slightly,
Home on the ground.
I shyly gave her the dollar that she took.
"God bless, thank your Mama."

A smile of some sort came from both sides,
But I was taken aback by it all.
I glanced back at my mom, feet away.

The crumbled-up dollar bill
Was no more than a stranger's to begin with.

Exhaustion

Take me now, I surrender.
Bring me into bouts of torture, isolation, silence, and captivation.

Take me now, and do what you will by my own will.
Sleep deprivation, I give myself back to you.

Do with me what you will
And amidst the torture and sorrow, perhaps I will rest.

All I need is some rest in hopes that the day can be mine to take.

CHAPTER FOUR

Waking Up

Pre-Dawn

Pre-dawn
Light green
Still stings
Light hurts.

Twinkling light
From the night
So sleepy
It hurts.

Moon's out
Desire to howl
Night owl
Up at dawn.

Yellow comes
Creeps up
Wakes up
Slow birth.

Birds fly
Miles high
Eyes shed
Their sleepy filter.

Waking up
Takes time
Parting with
Nightlife.

Wounds

Leave my troubles at home:
Childhood adversities,
Learned helplessness,
Negative,
Disillusionment,
Incomprehensible sense of self.

The baggage
Is far too heavy;
Too blinding
Too rooted,
It pulls me aloof.

I'm tired,
So tired,
Of living a beautiful life
With scales over my eyes.

I pick the scales off,
One by one,
But the wounds are still healing,
So deep and fragile.

The grey remains.
Darkness overtakes.
Life remains,
Keeps remaining,
A shadow;
Only a shadow.

Waterbed

So absorbed in self-acknowledgment that I begin to sink.
I'm not light like the air but heavy like the rushing waves.
My being is dense and frantic.
Even the calm shores hold dark waters beneath.

Sometimes I think it would be better to swim than to keep trying to float;
Getting over my comfort on this waterbed.
Emerging in the solidity of malleable matter, switching to a breaststroke.
I'd like to feel the water rise against my skin and actually propel myself by my own means.

Drive in Life

I want to live my life
In measures of aesthetics,
Not statistics.

To use my knowledge
Of compassion,
Not comparison.

To see the world
In shades deeper than color.

To look at the sunset
As a full-advantaged canvas,
And not just another act of nature.

To hear my own heart beating
And think it more than just
A heart
But what it holds
What I hold.

What each beat of my heart
Allows me:
Each breath
Each awakening

Falling asleep
And feeling content.

Measuring Life

Life moves so fast that it goes without you.
You feel time rush by in the wind but your mind stays in the moment
wondering how.

The happy moments fleet upon occurrence.
A carefree moment gets lost in the wind as soon as it comes.

Pick your head up from the ground.
You can't keep trying to hold on.

Intervening in My Own Life

All I do
Is watch from the sidelines.
Aware of my role
Always forgetting my lines.

I'm of stage fright,
I rather watch the play than play.
I can see how this will all end,
I see it end every day.

I can't help but curse the gods
Who wrote this goddamn script.
I plead with them to only make
A better ending to my fate.

Though hiding out of frame
Won't make this life of mine go away,
So on that idea alone
I'll make this life of mine my own.

Tree

A tree I stood
Still and quiet.
Observing and feeling
All the while being.

Birds would come
Sing and sit.
I'd feel their nails
Their little feet
Their beating hearts.

People would walk by
Dancing and laughing
Spinning and shivering
Admiring and pissing.

People would cry
Alone and ashamed
Looking around to ensure
No one is watching.

People passed
Some hugged me
Some cut me
Yet I remained.

The sun would come
And then she'd leave
Bring about seasons
Want a change in me.

Mother tested my limits
She'd let me burn and freeze.
She asked death to tempt me
Get close enough
Then leave.

I grew colder
But warmer still.
Come the spring,
I anticipated my bloom.
Feet higher, perhaps
But this year
I knew more
Had seen more
Had become more.

My rugged skin cracked
Atmosphere began to seep in.
The bark started to peel
Ripping away the facade
Like the waxing of a body.

Arms outstretched
Life in my fingers
I gave them a wiggle
A breath of life
The first one I feel.

My cage now shed
I join the field
Alone for now
But with time
I'll heal.

My feet lead me
My heart gives way.
Maybe I'll join
One of those people
One day.

The Language of Botany

Amid crumbling concrete castles and fixtures of stationary metals
beginning to rust
Life intrudes in camouflage across eroded lots.
As a hand reaches from the grave, the seeds and stems persist
Fighting for their share of life, something the grey resists.

Looking closer now, past the grey, directly to the green,
These sorts of structures aren't annual, or biennial, but evergreen.
Where nature strikes to scar the grey with lightning and the rage
of man,
The leaf scar soaks in the storm for a heart-shaped hug to its stalk.

We undermine the green.
We, like them, must fight for life to see.
Speaking another language, we can't hear their plea,
Yet in our own roots is the language of botany.

Alien

You're not of this world, you know.
Notice how you tremble in the cold
And how you fear what lies in the dark.

You pant in the beating heat
But it doesn't help to be engulfed in the waves.
Looking up doesn't do much good
You strain yourself from the longing.
The stars are too far out, another world away,
And the moon is so far out of reach,
You even lose it some nights.

The dirt rests close, earth underneath you.
This earth is yours, you know.
Both you and the trees grow.

Watch the birds fly up from the ground.
They soar the skies with your heart.
It comes back to the ground, it all.
The snow's a blanket and the sun a comforter.
You may not feel at home, but your roots run deep here.

Infra-Ordinary

When he calls me extraordinary, he has no idea
I want to be more. I want to be less.

When he takes my hand, he doesn't feel for the radial loop patterns on
all but three fingers
Or notice how my heartline tells him more of my sensitive side than
he could ever find.

While others yell louder than the thunder and shine brighter than its
astounding light,
I'd like for him to notice I'm more like the heartbeat of a puddle
brought to life by the falling rain.

I want his eyes to open and veer away from the main attraction amid
the show,
To notice the minuscule, like a penny heads-up on the floor.

I don't want to be the headlines or the dramatic face of any billboard,
But instead, the letters each is composed of: a single line in the grand
scheme of things.

I want to be the pace he walks as the world around us burns:
Never needing to be anything more, never really ending up as less.

At My Best

Meet me where the sun sets,
When I alone walk into the water
And begin to blend with the reflection
That sky makes on Earth.

Meet me in the crowded pines
With sky-high treetops and a peeking sun.
When I look up to see their heights
I won't look so small there alone on their roots.

Meet me on my solo drives.
Accompany me in the search for my soul.
Hear me out when I scream to you a song.
Be with me when I'm truly alone.

Who Am I?

Who am I but sadness—
A burden to carry in the pit of one's stomach?

Who am I but disappointment—
Never amounting to enough?

Who am I but guilt—
Weighing on one's shoulders?

Who am I but despair—
A hollow heart and heavy tears?

Who am I but love—
Overcoming all of these?

Shedding

And I could feel the sadness slip from me
Like I was shedding that skin.

CHAPTER FIVE

Redemption

Growing

I knew from the first kiss
There was something new in love.
To hold me and spin me around
In the pool that summer night
Showed me I don't know everything—
Not even close—about this life.

My horizon was broadened
And with open arms, you came.
When the months went by
And winter came home
I grew colder as I do.
The audacity of my mind
Told me I was right
To have not pursued you.

My days went on
As they do
As I dug deeper into the pit of me.
You won't be allowed to love me.

As I lay crying on the frozen sea,
New Year's Eve is dead to me,
The sun goes down its one last time
And again I'm forced to say goodbye.
Another year with its bitter end
Where no new things come as good
And you should know for certain
The clouds covered you
From my mind those nights.

I've told you before
In brief honesty
Why it is I hang on:
That giving up would disappoint
The ones whom I should love.
Suddenly you came
To mind that night.

I find it strange how the darkness keeps you away.
I know the days the sun shines light
Easier weather will move in.
So I suppose that's why in the spring
You came back to me.
Now that the air has lost its sting
And the rain replaces the snow,
We laugh in the thunderstorms.

The nights are still cold
But you love to build a fire and hold me close.
You are a protector,
Someone I am glad to have.
You will be there for me forever
I've learned
Only if I can learn to ask.
I'm growing warmer in your arms.
Learning about life and love
Growing up beside you.

Vibrant Blood

Sweetly sweetly sweetly
You came in to hold me
The transition of fright
By the unknown of a new embrace
Never wanting more power before
Than to hold so tightly onto
Each moment experienced with you.

Slowing time
Aging me around the years
Spent in the seconds with you.
A blink of the eyes,
A single kiss,
Will wrap me in an infinite.

These moments will make me,
Wash away the tainted grey
Of heartbreak and failed hope.
These moments will shape me,
Letting love take refuge
In my heart.

Your love will mend my mind,
Confused by design,
And the grey matter will shine
Red with vibrant blood.
Lighting up synapses of
Astonished understanding
Rewiring and reworking
Of misconceptions and second chances.

The claim you take on my
Brain will be that of
A renovator,
Redesigner,
Provider.
It is so much lighter
With you on my mind.

The Devil

I kissed the devil
Last night in my dreams
Instead of you.

Though I knew
Your touch holds me securely,
Your eyes see straight into mine,
His familiar lips leaned in
And a dance excited inside of me;
Feeling his warm breath
Salivating over his sweet lips.

So, I kissed the devil
Last night in my dreams
Instead of you.

His toxic grip on my heart
Makes it beat deeper,
Heavier, stronger.

I plead for release
It happens through a kiss
Then I get thrown
Back down to the ground.

So, darling, I kissed the devil
Last night in my dreams
Instead of you.

You have every right
To damn me to hell
Ridden of love
Starving of your touch.

But baby, I've woken up
From these nightmares
And in this new day
I want to relearn love
The way you love me,

Angelically.

Goodbye

Every empty hug
Engaged in for years on end
Convinced me time and time again
No one will make me feel.

The glimpses I'd catch
Felt like worlds unlocked.
So close to love's door,
But I never knew
The unimaginable
Until I met you.

Can you remember
What love was to you
Before you knew it?

I never wanted more,
Convinced nothing was enough,
Having walls so high
That my own mother's touch
Seemed lifeless.

But then I met love,
Really got to know her,
During the bittersweet
End to it all.

Through you
I learned to cry happily
To love drastically
To know I can.

The door you opened,
The world you gave me,
Was the most beautiful
Catastrophe
That the end of all things
Could have met.

Old Jewelry

The gift is here
Now
In your trembling fingers
Unraveled eagerly
Thoughtlessly
Wantingly.

The beauty in jewelry,
Besides its flashy face,
Is the life it lives
Long after ours.

The miles it has traveled
From you and our past
Felt by other lovers
Gazed upon by devil's eyes.

The sentiment of our love
Molded into shiny metal
Outlived the days you'd call me yours.

A piece of you remains
In this golden heart;
How could I forget you?

Before

I've met you before.
We've been together years before
We ever held a single conversation.
You were my rock once before, I'm sure.
We've had countless sleepovers
And forgotten sleepless nights.

It ended, it had to have
But you never broke my heart in the traditional way.
The déjà vu tells me I let you down.
It was never you who hurt me,
Just the lack of.

I'm glad you've come back to me
In this life.
I think somehow I grew into something better
This time.
The tragedies of this lifetime shaped me
Into something less of me and more of you.

This is how it was all supposed to go
When the cosmos realigned for this attempt.
And it's lovely so
That the reincarnation doesn't erase all of who I was before.
Although I cannot remember the world in which we've met before,
The emotions were surely pure enough to transcend to the now.
And now I will love you better than ever before.

Somebody

Somebody held me through the night
Somebody told me it was alright
Somebody asked me how it felt
And I told them.

Somebody made it work
For once
Somebody showed me they loved me.

They let me break
They let me fall
They took me in.

Somebody made
That lonely feeling
Start to fill, making a fix.

Somebody did that for me.

Something Sweeter

To have awoken
From an easy-going slumber
With dreams of papers and numbers,
The busy work that fills my days,
I open my eyes to see something sweeter
Lying there next to me.

How backward to dream of regular life
Only to awake into something much more?

Good to Know

You showed me understanding
In a way I never could.

Each conversation with you
Was a lesson to me
On how beautiful people can be.

The consideration of your words
And kind heart leaking through them
Coaxed me to believe in love
A bit more than I had always wished.

Late Night Conversations

Isn't it incredible that two people
With completely different stories
Find a way to perfectly understand each other
For a moment like this?

Real Love

An explosion
New life budding
Metamorphosis turning
Tangled in your love.

Sweetness seeping
From your kiss
Sliding down my throat
Soaking into my heart.

Each beat stronger
More assured
Now supported
It leaps with yours.

Our bodies dance
We push and pull
Give and take
To be with you.

Our fingers reach
Interlock and weave
Like ideas and feelings
On the tips of our tongues.

Your smile pulls each corner
Of my mouth apart
As a mirror of yours.

I want to rest inside of you
Nestle in your heart.

Thank God

What kind of Angel
Tells you they think you are?
What kind of Angel
Says you've answered their prayers?

To be loved by you
Is a blessing alone,
But to experience your Heaven
Seems too much to ask.
For what have I done
To deserve any of it?

I've never been the strongest believer,
Although now I know I've been mistaken.

Your touch is cloud nine
Yet I've never felt more grounded.
You've awoken parts of myself
That I didn't know were asleep.
You've given the fairytale of love
A playground to make proof
And shown me
What exactly it is
That God meant for us
When He made this whole thing.

The love I've always longed for,
Wanted so badly to be real,
Has a name now
And it's you.

Fairytale

He makes me warm,
Takes me home,
Sits me down,
And reads to me.

I lay on his chest
His arms around me
And my back is melting
Into his heart.

He holds the book
And opens it
One of which
Is oddly familiar
Yet this story
I never knew.

He reads to me
And tells me of
This once upon a time.

I isolate;
Try to relate,
But my storybook
Is no fairytale.

He tells me that
The princess is saved.
She finds her prince
And is okay.

The story settles
Then dissolves
From imagination
To something palpable.

He tells me of love
And I feel it.
He tells me of dreams
And I begin to live them.
He tells me of a happily ever after
And we make guesses
On how ours will go.

He slips the bookmark in
Holding me still in an embrace
And we drift away to a dream.

Stranger

Stranger, who are you?
Who are you to take my eyes away
From all I knew
And show me something more —
Much kinder, much sweeter?

Who are you to tango
With my words,
To rest assurance on
The small of my back
As you dip me,
Pulling me in
With a tender flow of natural love
Which I've never known.

Stranger, who are you?
Let me dig into your heart
And nestle a home.
Stranger, take me in.

Let the unknown infinity between us begin.
Keep my breath much longer.
Hold it, please, so that I may chase
After all I've hoped for,
Wished for,
In an embrace.

Taffy

I got into your car for the first time.
The unregistered voice of your first words to me
Shocked the skin of my ears, but melted softly into my head.
A voice like taffy, malleable and gentle, sweet and to chew on.
Your aroma became a closed-door atmosphere that you left unlocked
for me.
I wasn't nervous to enter.
The candy river swept me in.
And I didn't think twice about closing the door behind me.

Swerving

As we begin to drive home
You put on a song to show me.
The instrumental opens for you
And suddenly your heart is strung out into the air.

You sing out, eyes closed and all,
As the music surrenders to your voice.
Nothing escapes us there,
The blowing wind only adds more to it.

I'm locked in your harmony
Watching you feel so much.
You're not a distraction but a showcase.

I start to swerve, eyes off the road,
But there's no way you notice,
You're swaying side to side yourself
Melody like honey coming from your singing lips.

Darkroom Mind

Open shutter
Capturing the blur
Of moving people
Moving on
Moving away.
My pupils dilate;
They twitch at the weight
Of all there is to hold in.

My darkroom mind
Operates like a factory,
Understaffed and overworked,
In desperate attempt
To make sense
Of all I see.

The processes are precise
With time of the essence,
As I stand here and see you
Your photo develops wrong.
I blink on and off
To reset
But you are just so dark.

The staff buzzes
Around my cluttered mind
Holding up the line
Just to see you right.
They dodge and burn
Segments of photo paper
Trying to brighten
Your eyes
And fill the shades
Of your colored cheeks.

You are a piece of art;
A masterpiece of a portrait.
You're something
Anyone would frame
And hold high.

The night falls
And darkness enters
From outside the walls.
There you are: glowing,
No longer underexposed
But iridescent.
Under the sun's reflection
On the waning moon,
You stand there
Like all I'm meant to do
Is capture you.

Shadow

I'm glad my shadow has company;
The image is endearing,
Empty figures so full of feeling.
Mine's been alone for quite a while,
Chasing off those who might want to hold it.

It wanders, I've realized, far away
Even from myself at times.
Latching onto surfaces beyond me,
Disappearing into the shadows of my mind,
Resurfacing at my loneliest times.

And I forget she's there, other times,
Because she's always been so silent.
But to see her happy does me so much good,
To know that she now has a reason
To always come back.

Shall I Compare Thee to a Spring's Day?

If love is the weather, you are Spring's day,
Warmer and wiser than its lovesick air.
The birds want to repeat all that you say:
Singing to the flowers, your voice they share.

For this season I've waited all year long.
You've brought showers of change and things anew.
By your side seems best for where I belong.
For all you do, Angels look up to you.

With true beauty of the season comes Fall
When you leave me to remember it all.

Metamorphic

Are you still afraid to show me your wings?

They are so beautiful
Though broken,
Battered wings can still fly.

You hide away
In your metamorphosis.

The dark means more
Than an entrapment,
A cell,
But a cocoon.

And yet you stay there
So unaware
Of this glow;
You illuminate
Radiate
Bring light —
Make it.

And perhaps that's why
You're so full
Of something outer-worldly.

You've drafted hope when you were caged;
You brought light out of the dark —
And set free, you fly cautiously
In your own world
Afraid
Dusk will settle back down.

Don't you know by now
There are no gates that can hold you
Anymore?

Heaven Here

I see Heaven here
In the way the Earth spins
And the waves keep coming back to shore.

I see it here in the way the horizon line
Fogs over, converging Earth and sky.
Reflections on the water rock each other still,
Where the broken rocks fall and continue to lay,
The shore comes back and hugs them.

I see the trees giving standing ovations
And the seagulls starting to dance.
The wind tickles me to laugh a bit harder
And a smile rises like the sun.

Cognizance

Blissful air circulates my mind
A delightful atmosphere unlike the time
Spent under pressure, away in the dark
Cellar of cool, damp basement thoughts.

The friction of indecision fueling my anxious kind
Left grasping, guessing, all of the time.
Now blissful air circulates my mind.

Seasons

I look around
At the river, roots, and trees.
Even through the seasons
It's funny to say that what changed the most
Is me.

New Perspective

You don't know me like the sky
Watching over me for years gone by.
You tell me you're right here
But only the shores have held me dear.
You were never there, not in sight,
So I began looking up to be alright.

The night sky full of twinkling lights
Gives me perspective of new heights.
Now the stars ease my solitude,
Though the lights are a multitude,
In a community beyond our own
Perhaps here I have found a home.

Far away from it all, I feel alright;
Distance shows the stars most bright.
Far away but never closer
I feel some sadness lift with this closure.
Right at the edge of land, the start of the sea
I learn of things I never knew to be.
Something about the rushing waves
Teaches me how darkness behaves.
With a breath in I am with each splash
I feel a release with each crash.

The rain knows me by name
And each storm is the same
Welcoming me back
Proposing what I lack.
Alone I stand at the edge of land
Learning to hold my own hand.

Circles

Where I will end where I began,
Sleepy eyes welcoming a world anew.
Breaking out of each familiar cage
Knowing there's more;
Walking upon the stage
With more soul than I had last scene
Finding with time more reason to believe.

Seeking that every day I may grow
So I may never be made still;
Never restless but striving.
Conquering calm amid the storm
Letting each droplet sink in
And give back what was given.

May the sunlight shed light
Upon the darkness above my eyes
And melt the cold walls
That barricades this fragile heart.
The water will hug my tough skin
And allow me to indulge
Deeper than I ever could.

To float above the messy sea
Of thoughts and sunken feelings
And surface again on this earth
On the brink of a circular life

www.ingramcontent.com/pod-product-compliance
Lightning Source LLC
Chambersburg PA
CBHW051828040426
42447CB00006B/422